A

Symbols of American Freedom

Fort McHenry

by Michael Burgan

Series Consultant: Jerry D. Thompson,
Regents Professor of History,
Texas A&M International University

CHELSEA CLUBHOUSE

An Imprint of Chelsea House Publishers

Chelsea Clubhouse
An imprint of Chelsea House Publishers
132 West 31st Street
New York NY 10001

Library of Congress Cataloging-in-Publication Data
Burgan, Michael.
        Fort McHenry / by Michael Burgan.
            p. cm.
        Includes index.
        ISBN 978-1-60413-520-6
        1. Fort McHenry (Baltimore, Md.)—Juvenile literature. 2. Fort McHenry National Monument and
        Historic Shrine (Baltimore, Md.)—Juvenile literature. 3. Baltimore (Md.)—Buildings, structures,
        etc.—Juvenile literature. 4. Baltimore (Md.)—History, Military—Juvenile literature. I. Title.
        E356.B2B87 2010
        975.2'6—dc22   2009013340

Chelsea Clubhouse books are available at special discounts when purchased in bulk quantities
for businesses, associations, institutions, or sales promotions. Please call our Special Sales Department
in New York at (212) 967-8800 or (800) 322-8755.

You can find Chelsea Clubhouse on the World Wide Web at http://www.chelseahouse.com

Developed for Chelsea House by RJF Publishing LLC (www.RJFpublishing.com)
Text and cover design by Tammy West/Westgraphix LLC
Maps by Stefan Chabluk
Photo research by Edward A. Thomas
Index by Nila Glikin

Photo Credits: 5: © Paul A. Souders/CORBIS; 6: Smithsonian Institution Archives, Record Unit 95, image #MAH19703a; 7, 15: © Bettmann/CORBIS; 8, 34: AP/World Wide Photos; 11: National Archives, Records of the War Department, Cartographic Section, RG 77, drawer 51, sheet 1. Reproduced in HABS MD, 4-BALT, 5-14; 12: Library of Congress LC-USZ62-54696; 18: The Granger Collection, New York; 21, 41: © William S. Kuta/Alamy; 22, 33: Courtesy of the Maryland Historical Society; 24: North Winds Picture Archives/Alamy; 25: © Peter Harholdt/CORBIS; 27: Collection of the Maryland State Archives/Artist: Katherine Walton (d. 1938), Title: Francis Scott Key (1780-1843), Date: 1912, Medium: Oil on canvas, Dimensions: 30 x 24", Accession number: MSA SC 1545-1080; 29: Library of Congress LC-DIG-hec-04309; 31: Library of Congress LC-USZC2-3796; 32: Library of Congress LC-USZC4-1736; 35: National Park Service; 37: © Digital Vision/Alamy; 42: The American Flag Foundation, Inc.

Printed and bound in the United States of America

Bang RJF 10 9 8 7 6 5 4 3 2 1

This book is printed on acid-free paper.

All links and Web addresses were checked and verified to be correct at the time of publication. Because of the dynamic nature of the Web, some addresses and links may have changed since publication and may no longer be valid.

Note: Quotations in the text are used essentially as originally written. In some cases, spelling, punctuation, and the like have been modernized to aid student understanding.

Table of Contents

Words that are defined in the Glossary are in **bold** type
the first time they appear in the text.

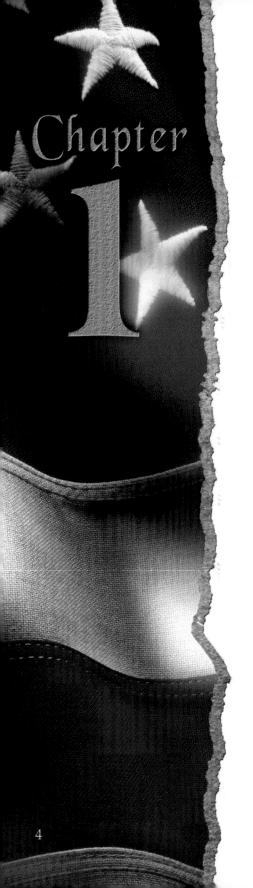

1

A Fort and Its Flag

Francis Scott Key stood on the deck of a ship in Baltimore Harbor. It was September 13, 1814. The United States and Great Britain had been at war for more than two years. British forces had just recently invaded and burned the U.S. **capital** of Washington, D.C. Now, Key watched as the British tried to take the nearby city of Baltimore, Maryland, as well.

The Banner Still Waves

All day on September 13, the British fired rockets and **shells** at Fort McHenry. The fort had helped guard Baltimore since 1802. The British hoped to destroy the fort so that their soldiers could easily enter the city. The attack lasted into the night. Key saw the red streaks of the rockets against the dark sky. He watched the bombs explode. He then looked through a telescope and saw a large U.S. flag flying over Fort McHenry.

All day and into the night on September 13–14, 1814, British ships fired on Fort McHenry, but they were not able to destroy or capture the fort.

Early in the morning of September 14, while it was still dark, the British shelling stopped. When daylight came, Key once again studied the sky over Fort McHenry. The flag that was sometimes called the Stars and Stripes still flew over the fort. The American soldiers there had survived the British attack.

Key was proud to see the U.S. flag still flying. He was impressed by the brave soldiers who helped defend Fort McHenry. On the ship, Key began writing some lines for a poem. He described what had happened during the battle. He finished the poem a few days later. Key's words were then set to the music of a popular song. Soon, people called his words and the music they were sung to "The Star-**Spangled** Banner." Today, Americans also call the song the National Anthem.

The Flags of Fort McHenry

The U.S. flag in 1814 had 15 red and white stripes. Each stripe stood for one of the states in the **Union** as of 1792. The flag also had 15 stars. In 1818, **Congress** decided not to add new stars and stripes for the new states that had joined the Union between 1794 and 1818. Today, the U.S. flag has 13 red and white stripes. They stand for the original 13 states. The current flag also has one star for each of the 50 states.

In September 1814, Fort McHenry had two large flags. The one that Francis Scott Key saw during the battle was called a storm flag. This version of the Stars and Stripes was 17 feet (5 meters) high and 25 feet (7.6 meters) long. The flag he saw after the battle was even larger. That flag measured 30 feet (9 meters) high and 42 feet (13 meters) long.

The large flag that Francis Scott Key saw on the morning after the battle was put on display outside the Smithsonian Institution in Washington, D.C., in 1914. The flag can be seen today inside the museum.

6

A Fort for All Time

Today, Fort McHenry is best known for its role during the fighting of September 13–14, 1814. That battle was part of a conflict now called the War of 1812. The fort also had many uses after that war. Fort McHenry continued to defend Baltimore and its harbor from possible attacks. Troops were based there into the twentieth century. At different times, the fort also served as a prison and as a hospital.

Then, in 1925, Fort McHenry was made a national park. Later, it was named a national **monument** and historic **shrine**. A shrine is a place that is considered to have special importance because of past events there.

Each year hundreds of thousands of visitors now come to Fort McHenry to learn about the fort's importance during the War of 1812. That war helped

Fort McHenry still sits at the entrance to Baltimore's harbor—with an American flag still flying over it.

In Their Own Words

Key's Poem

Not many Americans know all of Francis Scott Key's poem. Today, most people sing only the first verse, or part, of the National Anthem. Here are the complete words to the song:

Oh, say can you see by the dawn's early light
What so proudly we hailed at the twilight's last gleaming?
Whose broad stripes and bright stars thru the perilous fight,
O'er the ramparts we watched were so gallantly streaming?
And the rockets' red glare, the bombs bursting in air,
Gave proof through the night that our flag was still there.
Oh, say does that star-spangled banner yet wave
O'er the land of the free and the home of the brave?

On the shore, dimly seen through the mists of the deep,
Where the foe's haughty host in dread silence reposes,
What is that which the breeze, o'er the towering steep,
As it fitfully blows, half conceals, half discloses?
Now it catches the gleam of the morning's first beam,
In full glory reflected now shines in the stream:
'Tis the star-spangled banner! Oh long may it wave
O'er the land of the free and the home of the brave!

And where is that band who so vauntingly swore
That the havoc of war and the battle's confusion,
A home and a country should leave us no more!
Their blood has washed out their foul footsteps' pollution.
No refuge could save the hireling and slave
From the terror of flight, or the gloom of the grave:
And the star-spangled banner in triumph doth wave
O'er the land of the free and the home of the brave!

Oh! thus be it ever, when freemen shall stand
Between their loved home and the war's desolation!
Blest with victory and peace, may the heav'n rescued land
Praise the Power that hath made and preserved us a nation.
Then conquer we must, when our cause it is just,
And this be our motto: "In God is our trust."
And the star-spangled banner in triumph shall wave
O'er the land of the free and the home of the brave!

8

The Home of Fort McHenry

Baltimore, Maryland, was founded in 1729. The city sits on the Patapsco River. This river flows into Chesapeake Bay, which goes into the Atlantic Ocean. Baltimore's location helped it become a center for trade. In colonial days, ships from Baltimore sailed to other colonies and to islands in the Caribbean Sea. Some also went to Europe. By the time the War of 1812 started, Baltimore was the third-largest city in the United States. Today, Baltimore is still a major port. Ships from around the world bring their cargo there.

The National Anthem is played and sung at the beginning of sports events. Here, Jennifer Hudson sings "The Star-Spangled Banner" at the 2009 Super Bowl.

the United States keep the independence it had won just a few decades before in the American Revolution (1775–1783). The fort reminds people of the bravery of U.S. soldiers during the War of 1812. Visitors also learn about the role Fort McHenry played in the creation of the National Anthem—and about the roles it continued to play later in American history.

Preparing for War

The United States won its independence from Great Britain in 1783. Americans knew that one day they might have to defend themselves from enemy attacks. In 1794, the U.S. government decided to build a string of forts along the Atlantic coast. Baltimore was one of the cities chosen to receive a fort.

Work began on the Baltimore fort in 1798. The new fort was built on the site of an old fort called Fort Whetstone. The new fort had five sides. At each corner where the sides met, the walls formed a point, like an arrow. By 1802, the main brickwork at the site was complete. The first troops began to arrive. Baltimore's new fort was called Fort McHenry.

Troubles at Sea

Defending U.S. ports like Baltimore was important for the U.S. **economy**. Americans

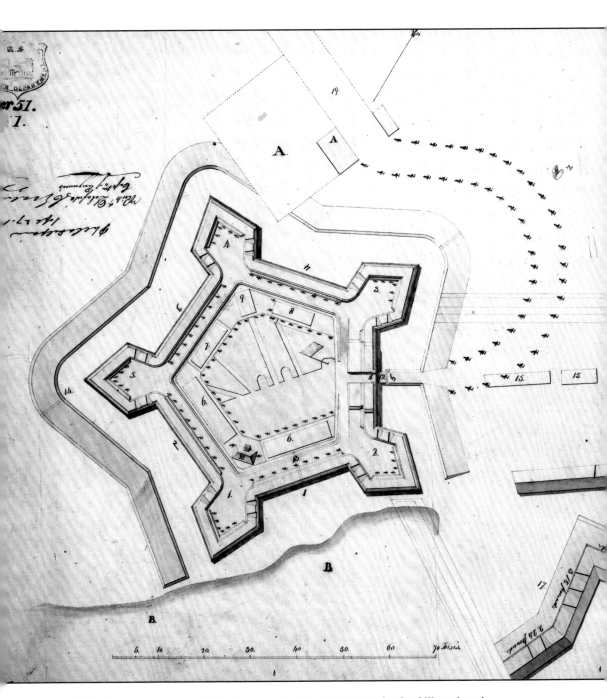

This drawing made in 1803 shows what Fort McHenry looked like when it was first built.

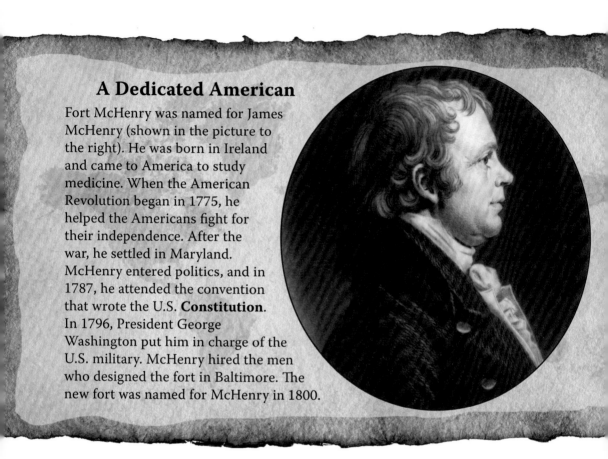

A Dedicated American

Fort McHenry was named for James McHenry (shown in the picture to the right). He was born in Ireland and came to America to study medicine. When the American Revolution began in 1775, he helped the Americans fight for their independence. After the war, he settled in Maryland. McHenry entered politics, and in 1787, he attended the convention that wrote the U.S. **Constitution**. In 1796, President George Washington put him in charge of the U.S. military. McHenry hired the men who designed the fort in Baltimore. The new fort was named for McHenry in 1800.

made money selling their goods overseas. U.S. ships carrying these goods traveled around the world. At times, some of these ships were stopped by the British Navy. The British wanted to search for sailors who had **deserted** British ships. The British seized any deserters they found on U.S. ships. At times, they also took sailors who were U.S. citizens and made them serve on British ships. This practice was called impressment, and it angered many Americans.

The British also upset Americans by trying to stop U.S. trade with France. Britain and France were at war in the early 1800s. The British did not want their enemy to receive U.S. goods. France also tried to restrict U.S. trade with Britain. Both countries sometimes stopped American ships, but Britain had a larger navy. The actions of the British Navy hurt the U.S. economy more.

In 1807, the U.S. government tried to punish Britain by cutting off all foreign trade. The law was also meant to hurt France. The U.S. **embargo**, however, hurt Americans merchants more than the British or French. The embargo ended in 1809, but Congress still limited American trade with Britain and France.

In 1809, James Madison became president. He did not want to fight a war with Britain. He and his supporters, however, believed the United States had to defend its rights. U.S. ships should be allowed to travel freely and not be stopped. U.S. and British **diplomats** met several times to try to end the disagreements between their countries. They never could.

Calls for War

By 1811, some U.S. officials wanted to go to war with Britain. They were angry over the British impressments. They also thought the British were helping Native Americans living to the west of the most settled areas of the United States. These Native Americans sometimes clashed with U.S. settlers moving west. Finally, some Americans thought a war could help

The *Chesapeake* Incident

The U.S. embargo came after a clash at sea. In June 1807, the British claimed that some sailors on the U.S. ship *Chesapeake* were deserters. The captain of the British ship *Leopard* wanted to search the *Chesapeake*. The U.S. captain said no. The British then fired on the *Chesapeake*, killing three sailors. The British came onboard and took away four men. The incident angered many Americans. They remembered this act of violence for years to come.

Slow News Is Not Good News

In 1812, the world did not have telephones or other ways of sending messages quickly. Some historians suggest that the War of 1812 might not have happened if such ways had existed. Congress declared war on June 18. Two days before, Great Britain said it would stop restricting U.S. trade. Americans, however, did not learn this for several weeks. The message had to come by ship across the Atlantic Ocean. Members of Congress might not have declared war if they had known about the British action.

the United States grow. If the country won, it might be able to take some or all of Canada from Britain. Members of Congress who wanted to fight the British were sometimes called "War Hawks."

In June 1812, President Madison asked Congress to declare war on Great Britain. He said that the U.S. right to trade freely was under attack. Madison believed the British were already acting as if they were at war with the United States. To some Americans, this new struggle was like a second war for independence. The country had to defend its rights against the British.

Battlefield Wins and Losses

The United States was not ready to fight a war. The nation had few trained solders and only three large warships. Americans were also split on waging a war at all. The New England states opposed the war. Governors there refused to send local **militia** to help U.S. troops. Still, Madison and the War Hawks thought they could win.

British-controlled Canada became the first U.S. target. The Americans tried to attack in three different areas. Each attack failed. Many of the battles took place near and on the Great Lakes. After one battle in January

1813, the British took about 500 prisoners. Hundreds more U.S. troops had been killed or wounded.

Still, the United States had some victories. In August 1812, the U.S.S. *Constitution* sank a British warship. In September 1813, Captain Oliver

Captain Oliver Hazard Perry (holding sword) had to be rowed to a different ship after his first one was damaged, but he still led the American fleet to victory at the Battle of Lake Erie.

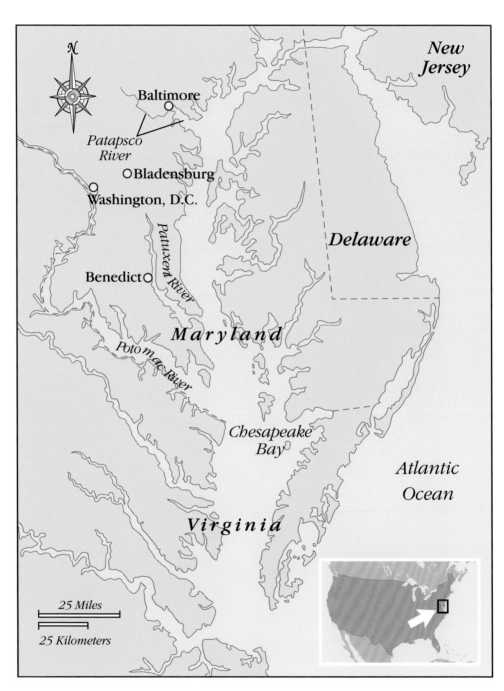

After their fleet entered Chesapeake Bay, British forces first attacked Washington, D.C. Then, they continued up Chesapeake Bay toward Baltimore.

Hazard Perry won a major naval battle on Lake Erie. Other U.S. victories came in what was then considered the West. In September 1813, General William Henry Harrison regained control of Detroit from the British. (British forces had captured Detroit in 1812.) The next month, Harrison defeated combined British and Native American forces in Canada.

On to Washington

During the War of 1812, the British were also fighting the French in Europe. The British and their **allies** defeated France in April 1814. The British then decided to send more ships and troops to North America. They began attacking U.S. towns and cities along the Atlantic coast. In July, the British forces headed for Chesapeake Bay. Their first target was the U.S. capital, Washington, D.C. British Admiral George Cockburn thought that taking the capital might weaken the Americans' desire to fight. He also wanted revenge. U.S. troops had recently set fire to some buildings in what is now the city of Toronto, Canada. Cockburn and other British officers wanted American cities to suffer in the same way.

"Old Ironsides"

The U.S.S. *Constitution* is one of the most famous American warships of all time. Its first major action in the War of 1812 came when it met the British warship *Guerriere* in the Atlantic Ocean east of Canada on August 19, 1812. In a sea battle in which the two ships fired their cannons at each other at close range, the *Constitution* succeeded in sinking the British ship and capturing most of its crew. At one point in the battle, a shot from a British cannon reportedly bounced off the side of the *Constitution*, earning the ship (which was really made of wood) the nickname "Old Ironsides." The *Constitution* went on to sink or capture several other British Navy ships during the War of 1812. It continued to sail for the U.S. Navy into the 1850s. Today, it is on display in Boston, Massachusetts.

In Their Own Words

A Capital in Flames

Colonel Arthur Brooke was one of the British soldiers who captured Washington, D.C. In his diary, he recorded what he saw:

"I think this was one of the finest, and at the same time, the most awful sights I ever witnessed—the columns of fire issuing from the houses, and the dock yard, the explosions of [stored gunpowder and shells]...the sky illuminated from the blazes."

The next morning, the British quickly left the city. Brooke wrote that the British could not believe "the Americans...would tamely allow a handful of British soldiers to advance through the heart of their country and burn and destroy the Capitol of the United States."

This illustration made shortly after the event shows British troops burning the city of Washington, D.C.

Books on Fire

The fire at the U.S. Capitol destroyed the Library of Congress. At the time, the library had about 3,000 books. Most were about history, law, and economics. Former President Thomas Jefferson loved books and had always supported the Library of Congress. He decided to help the library after the fire. Jefferson owned almost 6,500 books—more than any other American. He sold all of them to the Library of Congress. The new collection included books on the arts, science, and geography. Today, the Library of Congress occupies three buildings in Washington, D.C. The main building is named for Jefferson. The Library of Congress is the largest library in the world and has more than 138 million items.

On August 19, about 4,000 British troops landed at Benedict, Maryland. They marched for several days before they met U.S. forces on August 24. As the temperatures soared to 100°F (38°C), the two sides battled at the town of Bladensburg. The British forced the Americans to retreat toward Washington. The British soon followed them.

The Americans did not want to risk losing more men in Washington. They continued to retreat beyond the city. Residents began to flee the capital. They included President Madison's wife, Dolley. She took important papers, silverware, and other items from the White House. She wanted to make sure the British did not find them. She also ordered that a painting in the White House of George Washington be saved.

Washington was almost completely empty when the British troops arrived. They set fire to all the major public buildings. The first was the Capitol, where Congress met. Later, the British torched the White House. The fires burned through the night of August 24. By the next day, the British were gone. Americans living around Chesapeake Bay wondered where they would strike next.

The Rockets' Red Glare

Maryland had begun preparing for war back in 1813. That was when some British ships had first reached Chesapeake Bay. These ships sometimes raided towns along the coast. At that time, Baltimore had called for local militia to help defend the city. Regular army troops were also based at Fort McHenry. Throughout 1813, the militia and local residents built several new small forts in Baltimore. Fort McHenry, however, remained the most important defense for the city. Major George Armistead was in charge of the fort. He asked local men to join the army and serve there. By the time the British destroyed Washington in August 1814, Armistead commanded about 1,000 men. Fort McHenry was also defended by more than 50 pieces of **artillery**. Several thousand more troops in and around Baltimore were also ready to defend the city.

The men at Fort McHenry spent their days preparing for battle. They marched, stood

Cannons like this one were used to defend Fort McHenry and the city of Baltimore. In this present-day photo, people dressed as soldiers from the War of 1812 show how a cannon would have been moved within the fort.

on guard, and practiced firing the artillery. The **gunners** had a dangerous job. A cannon might accidentally explode, killing or wounding the soldiers nearby. Some gunners also lost their hearing because of the loud booms of the cannons. The gunners worked hard to improve their skills. Cannon-balls had to be loaded one at a time. The heaviest weighed 36 pounds (16 kilograms). A good artillery team could load and fire its gun four times in one minute.

The British Reach Baltimore

After destroying Washington, British officers debated where to go next. One wanted to attack Rhode Island, but several thought Baltimore should

Major George Armistead was in command at Fort McHenry when the British attacked.

be the next target. Some British officers called the city "a nest of pirates." Ships from Baltimore often attacked British ships that were carrying supplies. The officers wanted to make Baltimore suffer for the damage its ships had done. The British sailed for Baltimore on September 10, 1814.

By this time, all of Baltimore was ready for battle. More militia had come to the city. Local residents had dug trenches so that soldiers could protect themselves when the British attacked. Guns were ready at Fort McHenry and the other forts. Some artillery was also placed on boats in the harbor.

African Americans in the War

During the War of 1812, African-American slavery was an important part of the economy in the South. Maryland was one of the states in which many white people owned slaves. The British hoped to convince slaves to leave their masters and fight against the United States. Most, though, did not. In Baltimore, slaves helped defend the city from the British attack. One Maryland slave named William Williams ran away from his master and joined the U.S. Army. He served at Fort McHenry during the Battle of Baltimore. In the battle, Williams was hit by a British cannonball and lost his leg. He later died from his injury. Maryland also had free African Americans who fought the British during the war. Some of them served on ships that sailed out of Baltimore.

On September 11, the British ships sailed up the Patapsco River. Early the next morning, about 4,700 troops came ashore. The British planned to attack the city from both land and water. The U.S. militia and soldiers knew the British were coming. A U.S. officer ordered that American merchant ships be sunk near Fort McHenry. The wrecked ships would keep the British Navy from getting too close to the city. About 3,000 militia prepared to meet the British troops who were marching toward Baltimore. In Fort McHenry, the soldiers stood by the artillery. Above the fort, the storm flag flew in the breeze. Rain was falling.

The Battle of Baltimore began outside the city. The U.S. militia fired first on the advancing British troops. The two sides fought throughout the

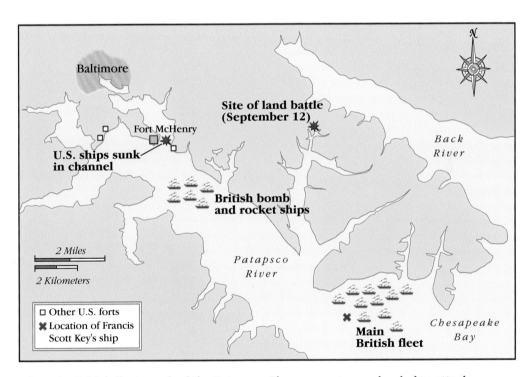

When the British fleet reached the Patapsco River, some troops landed to attack Baltimore by land. Some of the ships moved closer to the city. American ships had been sunk to block their way. And most important, Fort McHenry and its defenders stood between the British and Baltimore.

Smoke and flames can be seen in this picture, as the big guns on the British ships and in Fort McHenry fired on each other.

day on September 12. The Americans retreated as night fell. The British, however, suffered several hundred **casualties** and had not reached the city.

Bombs and Rockets over Baltimore

Early in the morning on September 13, the British began to attack Fort McHenry. The first shell came from the British ship *Volcano*. The bombs were meant to explode as they reached their target. The sailors, however, could not always get the timing right for the explosion. Some of the bombs burst while they were still sailing through the air. The British also fired rockets. The rockets were long tubes filled with gunpowder. They were designed to start fires when they landed. They did not often hit their targets, but they were good at scaring an enemy.

In Fort McHenry, Major Armistead's men fought back with their artillery. One U.S. cannonball ripped through the sail of a British ship. Then, the British moved their ships slightly farther away from the fort. Their guns could still hit Fort McHenry, but the U.S. artillery could not hit their ships. About 10 A.M., Armistead told his men to stop firing. The British, however, kept firing their rockets and shells. Most of them caused little damage in the well-built fort.

In the afternoon, the British finally scored a direct hit. A bomb struck the **magazine** where the Americans stored their gunpowder. A soldier

Baltimore Clippers

Baltimore was known for its skilled shipbuilders. The most famous ship made there was the Baltimore clipper. Clipper ships were faster than the ships the British used. During the War of 1812, many Baltimore sea captains, sailing in clipper ships, became **privateers**. They received permission from the U.S. government to stop British ships and seize their cargo. At times, they also sank the British ships. The privateers in their clipper ships could outrun British naval ships that chased them. The privateers were the "pirates" the British hated so much. Baltimore privateers captured more than 500 British ships during the war.

Baltimore clippers, such as the one shown here, were among the fastest ships of their time.

poured water on the bomb, and it did not explode. Two other British shots struck one of the fort's cannons. Several men were killed.

About 3 P.M., the British once again moved their ships closer to the fort. They thought the Americans were ready to give up since they had fired so few times. As the British approached, Armistead's men once again opened fire. Several British ships were hit. Once again, the British pulled back. They realized that the defenders of Fort McHenry were still ready to fight. As rain fell, the British continued to shell into the night.

A Distant Watcher

About eight miles (13 kilometers) away, Francis Scott Key heard the sounds of war. He and a U.S. official named John S. Skinner were on board a ship sitting in the Patapsco River. On September 7, the two Americans had sailed to the British ships, hoping to win the release of an American who was being held prisoner. The British agreed to release him. How-

In Their Own Words

A Sneak Attack

During the night of September 13, the British tried to sneak troops into Baltimore by boat. Francis Scott Key later wrote about the events that followed:

"Fort McHenry opened the full force of all her [guns] upon them…and the fleet responding with entire broadsides made an explosion so terrific…the heavens aglow were a seething sea of flame, and the waters of the harbor [were] lashed into an angry sea by the vibrations…. It is recorded that the houses in the city of Baltimore, two miles distant, were shaken to their foundations…. Suddenly, it ceased—all was quiet, not a shot fired or sound heard, a deathlike stillness prevailed…. The awful stillness and suspense were unbearable."

Lawyer and Poet: Francis Scott Key (1779–1843)

Francis Scott Key was born in 1779 in western Maryland. He was a successful lawyer when the War of 1812 began. His strong religious beliefs led him at first to oppose the war. He later served as an officer in the Maryland militia, however, and fought in the battle at Bladensburg. During the attack on Washington, D.C., the British arrested a Maryland doctor named William Beanes. Key won permission from President Madison to try to gain Beanes's release. Key wrote his famous poem while he watched the defense of Fort McHenry. After the War of 1812, Key once again practiced law. For several years, he served as a government lawyer in Washington, D.C. Key also began to oppose slavery. For a time he owned several slaves, but he freed them. Key also wrote other poems. They were collected into a book several years after he died in 1843.

ever, when the British decided to attack Baltimore, they would not let Key, Skinner, and the former prisoner go. They did not want the men to go back to the Americans and reveal the British plans to attack.

On September 13, Key used a telescope to watch the skies over Baltimore. He saw the storm flag flying over Fort McHenry. Then, as the rain continued to fall and the British guns stopped firing during the night, he could not see the flag. Key would have to wait for sunrise on September 14 to see if Fort McHenry had survived the fight.

4

Victory and After

Around 4 A.M. on September 14, almost all the firing stopped in Baltimore Harbor. The British had fired about 1,500 bombs and rockets at Fort McHenry but had failed to damage it. A few hours later, the British ships began to sail back down the Patapsco River. The British failure to take Fort McHenry was important for Baltimore. The British troops outside the city had been ready to attack again. Their commander, however, was afraid to fight without help from the guns on the British ships. By dawn, the British soldiers were also retreating. They would not attack Baltimore.

As morning came, Major Armistead took down the storm flag that had flown over the fort during the battle. He raised the larger flag instead. He wanted the British and everyone else to know that his men had won the battle. As the flag went up, the fort's band played "Yankee Doodle."

A Poem and a Song

The morning of September 14 was cloudy. From the ship he was on, Francis Scott Key had trouble seeing Fort McHenry. Finally, through his telescope he saw the large flag flying there. He knew the Americans had survived and saved the fort. Key began to write a poem to describe the battle he had seen and heard through the night. He finished it a few days later.

Key had not given his poem a title. A friend of his decided to publish the poem and hand it out in Baltimore. The friend called the poem "The Defense of Fort McHenry." Soon, Key renamed it "The Star-Spangled Banner." Key seems to have written the poem with a popular song in his mind. His words fit the tune of a song called "**Anacreon** in Heaven." Both the Americans and the British knew the song well. Key's poem was first sung to the music of that song in October 1814. Meanwhile, newspapers across the country printed the words to Key's poem. Americans

From Popular Song to National Anthem

After the War of 1812, Americans continued to sing "The Star-Spangled Banner." During the Civil War (1861–1865), both the North and the South played the song in public. By the 1890s, it was played by bands in the U.S. Army and Navy. An Italian opera composer used part of the song when an American character came on stage. He knew his audience would know the tune and connect it with the United States. In 1916, President Woodrow Wilson ordered that "The Star-Spangled Banner" be played at official government events. Congress made the song the country's National Anthem in 1931.

everywhere were proud of the victory at Fort McHenry. Key's words were a reminder of that event.

After the War

The War of 1812 ended soon after the Battle of Baltimore. U.S. and British diplomats had already been holding peace talks. Both countries were tired of the war. The two sides signed a treaty in December 1814. The war officially ended in February 1815.

President Madison knew the country could face future wars. He called for building new forts and improving the old ones. In 1817, workers began adding new walls at Fort McHenry. More important work began in 1829. Another story was added to buildings inside the fort. Over the next ten years, the fort received new guns and walls. More land was also added to the grounds outside the original fort.

The United States went to war again in 1846, this time with Mexico. The fighting took place much farther west. Troops were trained at Fort McHenry to fight in this war.

The Civil War

For decades, the nation had argued over slavery. Southern states favored slavery. Landowners used slaves to grow important crops, such as cotton and tobacco. Slaves also worked in homes and sometimes in businesses. Northern states, however, had begun to outlaw slavery in the late eighteenth century. Some people in the North wanted to end slavery everywhere. In 1860, South Carolina became the first slave state to secede, or leave the Union. Ten others soon followed. President Abraham Lincoln said these states did not have a legal right to secede. The Civil War was fought to keep the Union whole.

The Last Battle

In January 1815 in New Orleans, Louisiana, U.S. troops led by General Andrew Jackson defeated a large British force that was attacking the city. This victory came several weeks after British and U.S. diplomats had agreed to end the war.

Once again, slow communications played a role during the War of 1812. The news of the treaty did not reach the United States until after Jackson's victory.

Led by Andrew Jackson (standing, in blue uniform, and pointing his sword), American troops easily defeated a large British force at the Battle of New Orleans.

Union soldiers and people who supported the South clashed on the streets of Baltimore in 1861.

Maryland was in a difficult position during the Civil War. The state allowed slavery. Some Marylanders strongly supported the South and wanted to secede. Others did not. Baltimore was an important port, and now railroads also passed through the city. Because of this, President Lincoln and other Union leaders wanted to keep Baltimore under their control. The Union needed the city's harbor and railroads to make sure it

Prison Life

Civil War prisoners faced harsh conditions at Fort McHenry. They received only one blanket each and could not have chairs. They had tin cups and used forks and spoons they made out of wood. They received very little meat to eat, and it was often rotten. The prisoners could play baseball, however, and at night, they performed shows for each other. For a brief time in 1863, almost 7,000 prisoners were crammed into the fort.

Three prisoners at Fort McHenry were **executed** for their crimes. One Union soldier was executed for killing an officer. Another was killed for spying for the South. A Southern soldier was also executed for being a spy.

This photo shows the inside of Fort McHenry in 1890.

could move troops and supplies. In the end, Maryland decided to stay in the Union.

In April 1861, however, some Baltimore residents protested against the Union. The U.S. government sent men and artillery to Fort McHenry to keep order. The fort was also used as a prison. Some of the prisoners were Maryland residents who supported the South. Most were Southern soldiers captured on the battlefield.

An Aging Fort

After the Civil War, Fort McHenry received new guns. These were much larger than the old artillery used at the fort. The fort, though, lost some of its land. Baltimore was growing. Companies wanted land by the water to repair ships. The government gave up some land by the fort in 1878.

Fort McHenry slowly began to lose its military importance. The United States had built newer forts on the Patapsco River closer to Chesapeake

A Notable Resident

One famous military person to serve at Fort McHenry was Walter Reed (see photo to the right). He was an army doctor when he first arrived at the fort in 1881. Reed received permission to spend time away from the fort and study in Baltimore. He took classes at Johns Hopkins Hospital and studied the various causes of disease. Reed left Baltimore in 1882 but returned in 1890 and did more research. He later traveled to Cuba and helped explain how mosquitoes cause the disease yellow fever. The main U.S. Army hospital in Washington, D.C., is named for him.

Bay. The country was also less likely to be attacked by sea than it had been in 1812. The United States was building a powerful navy that could defend its shores. The nation did not have to rely on coastal forts.

In 1898, the United States fought a war with Spain. Fort McHenry was used as a base to train soldiers. About ten years later, members of the Coast Guard were sent there. They remained until 1912, when the government stopped using Fort McHenry as a base for troops. Still, the fort would have many uses in the years to come.

From City Park to National Monument

In 1914, the U.S. government let the city of Baltimore use Fort McHenry as a park. For a time, some of the land by the fort was used as a beach. By 1917, though, the United States was once again at war. The nation sent troops to Europe to fight in World War I. The U.S. government took back the fort and used it as an army hospital. Some wounded soldiers

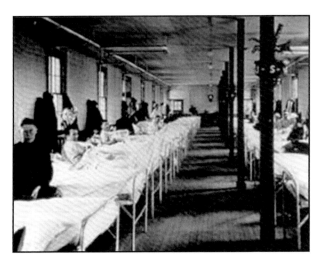

During World War I and for several years after the war, Fort McHenry was used by the army as a hospital for wounded and ill soldiers.

also took classes at the fort while they recovered. World War I ended in November 1918, but Fort McHenry remained a military hospital until 1923.

In 1925, the U.S. government named Fort McHenry a national park. Leaders wanted to honor the fort's role in the creation of "The Star-Spangled Banner." The government began to repair buildings inside the fort. Fort McHenry opened as a national park in 1928. Repair work went on for several more years. In 1939, the fort received a new title. That year, it became a national monument and historic shrine.

Another war gave Fort McHenry a new military role. The United States entered World War II in 1941. Baltimore factories built warplanes and ships for the military. The Coast Guard needed people to patrol the harbor area and watch for enemy activity. The government set up a training base on land outside Fort McHenry. Coast Guard crews at the fort also learned how to fight fires onboard ships. About 28,000 people were trained at the fort during the war.

World War II ended in 1945. Fort McHenry was soon a site for tourists, not soldiers or sailors. People came to learn about Fort McHenry's role throughout U.S. history. Scientists called archaeologists dug at the fort. They searched for clues about how the fort looked in the past. The fort also became a site for celebrations honoring the U.S. flag and "The Star-Spangled Banner."

Visiting Fort McHenry Today

I n 1964, the U.S. government opened a Visitor Center at Fort McHenry. The next year, a military band performed a concert at the fort for the first time. The National Park Service wanted more people to come to the fort and learn about its past. Those efforts have increased since then. Now, more than 600,000 people visit Fort McHenry each year. A new Visitor Center is expected to open in 2010 to welcome the many guests to Fort McHenry.

Visiting the Fort

Fort McHenry is about 2 miles (3.2 kilometers) from the center of Baltimore. The grounds of the fort cover 43 acres (17.4 hectares). Just beyond the fort is a picnic area. Nearby is a dock for boats.

The first stop for most people is the Visitor Center. Here, they can view a short film about the fort's history. The center also has exhibits explaining the fort's past. Outside the center is a statue of Major George Armistead, the fort's commander during the Battle of Baltimore.

Several parts of Fort McHenry were added after 1814. These include the first building that guests see as they near the fort. The building, which is called a ravelin, is shaped like an arrow. The ravelin was built to defend the entrance to the fort. Underneath it are rooms where supplies were stored. Visitors can explore the walkways and rooms under the ravelin.

Past the ravelin is an arch that leads into the fort. Inside, visitors explore on their own, but park rangers can offer details about the fort. The fort also has several markers that explain the events of 1814 and how the fort was built. One of them is near a British bomb that struck the fort during the battle. The bomb failed to explode. The bomb sits near a row of cannons similar to the ones the Americans had at the fort in 1814.

Going through the entrance, visitors pass two guardhouses. These buildings were added in 1835. Also near the entrance are buildings called bombproofs. They were built after 1814 to protect the fort's soldiers from

These large guns brought to Fort McHenry shortly after the Civil War can be seen by visitors today just outside the fort.

The Banner Then and Now

In 1813, Major Armistead hired Mary Pickersgill to sew a flag for Fort McHenry. She and her 13-year-old daughter, Caroline, along with two nieces and a servant, made both the storm flag and the larger banner that flew on September 14, 1814. When Major Armistead left the fort, he took the large banner with him. The flag remained in his family for many years. Some Americans wanted to own a small bit of the important flag, so at times, members of the Armistead family gave away pieces of the flag.

In 1912, Major Armistead's grandson gave the flag to the Smithsonian Institution in Washington, D.C. Workers at the museum have kept the flag from falling apart. The flag is now displayed in a special glass case to keep it safe.

enemy attacks. They were never used, since Fort McHenry was never bombed again.

Straight ahead through the entrance is the flagpole. The original large flag—the Star-Spangled Banner—that Francis Scott Key saw flew from this pole. A full-sized copy of that flag is now flown on the pole on summer days. A smaller flag with 50 stars is put up at other times. When a new U.S. flag is designed, it is first flown here before it is put into use. This act is meant to show a connection between the Star-Spangled Banner and today's flags.

Around the inside walls of the fort are several buildings. They were used as **barracks** for the men. Inside the barracks, visitors see exhibits about how the soldiers lived and worked. The men slept on bunk beds in small rooms. Officers had their own barracks. Major Armistead had his own building where he slept and worked.

Another building inside the fort was used to store gunpowder and cannonballs. This building replaced the one that was used during the War of 1812. A marker tells the story of the British bomb that hit the original magazine on September 13, 1814, but did not explode. Another marker describes the place where, during the Civil War, the fort's most dangerous prisoners were kept.

Outside the fort, visitors can see artillery that was put in place just after the Civil War. These weapons are called Rodman guns. They are named for the man who invented them. A marker explains the hard work it took for gunners to load and fire these guns.

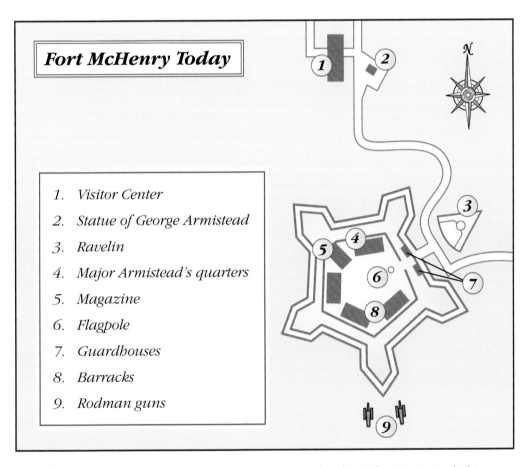

Fort McHenry Today

1. *Visitor Center*
2. *Statue of George Armistead*
3. *Ravelin*
4. *Major Armistead's quarters*
5. *Magazine*
6. *Flagpole*
7. *Guardhouses*
8. *Barracks*
9. *Rodman guns*

As visitors tour Fort McHenry, they can see the flagpole where the Star-Spangled Banner waved and buildings used by the soldiers defending the fort in September 1814. They can see later additions to the fort as well.

History Comes Alive

On weekends during the summer, visitors get a better idea of what life was like at Fort McHenry. A few dozen local residents form the Fort McHenry Guard. These men and women dress as people did in 1814 and pretend to be soldiers and city residents from that time. Some of the "soldiers" sit in the barracks. They explain to visitors how the soldiers of 1814 lived. Some of the soldiers clean their guns. Others take time from their chores to play checkers or cards.

Cooks display the kinds of foods the soldiers ate. The **re-enactors** also drill outdoors and fire cannons. Some play drums and **fifes**, as the fort's band did during the War of 1812. The military bands were used to signal the troops. A certain drumbeat told the troops what to do. The bands also played songs on special occasions.

The Guard members who play citizens show how the War of 1812 affected Baltimore residents. Women and children visited relatives at the fort. Merchants came and sold goods. Some women helped wash and sew clothes for the troops.

Playing a Part for History

People who join the Fort McHenry Guard receive special training. The soldiers must be able to fire working models of the guns and cannons used during the War of 1812. Re-enactors playing Baltimore residents learn how to do crafts that people did long ago. All the Guard members must be able to explain the history of the fort and the important events that took place there. They also discuss life in Baltimore before and after the war. The National Park Service pays for the clothes the re-enactors wear and the equipment they use at the fort. Sometimes, the Guard members travel to schools and public events to show their skills and tell about life at the fort in 1814.

Members of a group called the Fort McHenry Guard, who dress in uniforms like those worn in the War of 1812, can be seen by visitors to the fort.

Activities at Fort McHenry

The Fort McHenry Guard often takes part in special events held at the fort. Each year on September 12, Maryland celebrates Defenders Day. This holiday honors the soldiers who fought in the Battle of Baltimore.

The Living Flag

On September 14, 1914, Fort McHenry had its first Living Flag ceremony, sponsored by The American Flag Foundation. The date was exactly one hundred years after Francis Scott Key began writing "The Star-Spangled Banner." About 6,500 Baltimore schoolchildren helped make up the flag. They stood in precise spots and wore hooded sweatshirts colored red, white, or blue. The students also waved small pieces of cloth the same color as their sweatshirts. This made it look as if the "flag" were waving in the breeze. Living Flag ceremonies were also held at the fort each year from 1983 to 2008. Between 3,000 and 5,000 students took part in the ceremony, holding red, white, or blue cards.

The picture shows The American Flag Foundation's 2006 third-, fourth-, and fifth-graders' Annual Living American Flag event, held at Fort McHenry.

On the weekend closest to that day, the Fort McHenry Guard holds the Star-Spangled Banner Weekend. The soldiers pretend to fight re-enactors dressed as British soldiers. The weekend events also include parades, music, and fireworks.

Every summer, a number of concerts are held at Fort McHenry. They feature bands from the U.S. military playing patriotic songs. Fife and drum bands also sometimes appear. They play music that was popular during the War of 1812 and the Civil War. These bands also play at the fort's Fourth of July celebrations. During those celebrations, visitors can learn dances and games that were popular with people in the nineteenth century and can watch a fireworks display.

Several events at Fort McHenry mark its ties to the U.S. flag. June 14 is Flag Day, and a group called The American Flag Foundation has a celebration at the fort on that day. Visitors say the Pledge of Allegiance, then enjoy music and fireworks. On Memorial Day, the fort flies historic U.S. flags as part of ceremonies to honor the U.S. military.

Another special event in June is the Juneteenth celebration. June 19, 1865, was the day when slaves in Texas learned they were free. This happened about two months after the end of the Civil War. Fort McHenry celebrates the day by honoring important African Americans. The fort also has re-enactors dressed as Civil War soldiers and holds a reading of Abraham Lincoln's Emancipation Proclamation. That historic document, issued by President Lincoln on January 1, 1863, declared free the slaves living in the parts of the South that were in rebellion against the Union.

Even if there are no specials events, Fort McHenry offers visitors plenty to see. The fort played an important role in keeping the United States a free nation. The bravery of its troops in 1814 led to the writing of "The Star-Spangled Banner." The song and the flag it honors are important symbols for the country.

★ **1798** Work begins on Fort McHenry in Baltimore.

★ **1802** The first soldiers arrive at the fort.

★ **1807** A British attack on the U.S. ship *Chesapeake* angers many Americans. The U.S. government cuts off all foreign trade.

★ **1812** Congress declares war on Great Britain, starting the War of 1812.

★ **1814** **August:** British troops invade Washington, D.C., and burn most public buildings there. **September:** British troops begin a land attack on Baltimore, but the Americans hold them off. The British then begin to shell Fort McHenry. The British fail to take the fort. Francis Scott Key writes a poem that becomes the words to the song "The Star-Spangled Banner."

★ **1815** The War of 1812 officially ends.

★ **1861** The Civil War begins, and Fort McHenry is used as a prison.

★ **1898** During the Spanish-American War, soldiers train at Fort McHenry.

★ **1912** The government stops using Fort McHenry as a base for the U.S. military.

★ **1917** The United States enters World War I and turns Fort McHenry into a military hospital.

★ **1925** The U.S. government makes Fort McHenry a national park.

★ **1931** "The Star-Spangled Banner" becomes the U.S. National Anthem.

★ **1939** The fort is named a national monument and historic shrine.

★ **1942** After entering World War II in 1941, the U.S. government turns Fort McHenry into a training base and uses it until 1945.

★ **1964** Fort McHenry opens its first Visitor Center.

allies: People, groups, or countries that work together for a common goal, especially during wartime.

Anacreon: An ancient Greek poet.

artillery: Cannons and other large guns that fire cannonballs, shells filled with explosives, or other objects over long distances.

barracks: Buildings where groups of people sleep.

capital: The city or town that is the center of a state or country's government.

casualties: Soldiers who are killed, wounded, missing, or taken prisoner during a battle.

Congress: The branch of the U.S. government that makes the laws.

constitution: A document that outlines a country's or a state's form of government and how laws are made and enforced.

deserted: Left a military post without permission.

diplomats: Officials who help carry out their country's relations with foreign nations.

economy: A system of producing and distributing goods and services.

embargo: A ban on the trade of goods between countries.

executed: Killed as punishment for breaking a law.

fifes: Small flutes.

gunners: Soldiers who operate large guns.

magazine: A place where gunpowder and military supplies are stored.

militia: Citizens who train as soldiers and who fight when needed.

monument: A structure to remember a special person or event.

privateers: Privately owned ships that receive their government's permission to capture enemy ships; also, the sailors on those ships.

re-enactors: People who dress and act like people from the past to explain historical events.

shells: Exploding objects shot out of guns.

shrine: A place considered holy or special because of past events there.

spangled: Covered with small, shiny, or sparkling decorations.

Union: Another name for the United States.

To Learn More ★ ★ ★ ★ ★ ★ ★

Read these books

Ashby, Ruth. *James and Dolley Madison*. Milwaukee: World Almanac Library, 2005.

Edelman, Rob, and Audrey Kupferberg. *The War of 1812*. Farmington Hills, Mich.: Blackbirch Press, 2005.

Hess, Debra. *The Star-Spangled Banner*. New York: Benchmark Books, 2004.

Kjelle, Marylou Morano. *Francis Scott Key*. Hockessin, Del.: Mitchell Lane Publishers, 2007.

Landau, Elaine. *The National Anthem*. New York: Scholastic, 2008.

Maynard, Charles W. *Fort McHenry*. New York: Rosen Publishing, 2002.

Schultz, Randy. *Washington Ablaze: The War of 1812*. Vero Beach, Fla.: Rourke Publishing, 2007.

Look up these Web sites

The American Flag Foundation—The Living American Flag
http://www.americanflagfoundation.org/content/livingamericanflag.cfm

American Treasures of the Library of Congress—The Star-Spangled Banner
http://www.loc.gov/exhibits/treasures/trm065.html

The Fort McHenry Guard
http://www.fortmchenryguard.org

The National Anthem Project
http://www.tnap.org/index.html

National Park Service—Fort McHenry National Monument and Historic Site
http://www.nps.gov/fomc

The Star-Spangled Banner
http://www.americanhistory.si.edu/starspangledbanner

The War of 1812
http://www.history.army.mil/books/AMH/AMH-06.htm

Key Internet search terms

Battle of Baltimore, Fort McHenry, Francis Scott Key, National Anthem, Star-Spangled Banner, War of 1812

The abbreviation *ill.* stands for illustration, and *ills.* stands for illustrations. Page references to illustrations and maps are in *italic* type.

Index ★ ★ ★ ★ ★ ★ ★ ★ ★

★ ★

About the Author

Michael Burgan is a former editor at *Weekly Reader*, where he wrote about current events. As a freelance author, he has written more than 150 books for children and young adults, mostly nonfiction. His specialty is U.S. history and biographies of world figures. He is also a playwright. Burgan has a B.A. in history from the University of Connecticut and currently lives with his wife in Chicago.